**YOU'RE NOT AS GOOD
AS YOU THINK YOU ARE**

You're Not As Good As You Think You Are

A DEMOTIVATIONAL GUIDE

by
Chris Gudgeon
with "Sugar" Roy Carboyle

ARSENAL PULP PRESS
Vancouver

ARSENAL PULP PRESS
103-1014 Homer Street
Vancouver, B.C.
Canada V6B 2W9

The Publisher gratefully acknowledges the support of the Canada Council for the Arts for its publishing program, and the support of the Book Publishing Industry Development Program, and the B.C. Arts Council.

Typeset by the Vancouver Desktop Publishing Centre
Printed and bound in Canada by Webcom

CANADIAN CATALOGUING IN PUBLICATION DATA:
Gudgeon, Chris, 1959-
   You're not as good as you think you are

   ISBN 1-55152-040-0

   1. Success—Humor.   2. Self-help techniques—Humor.   3.
Canadian wit and humor, English.   I. Title.
PN6231.S83G82 1997   C818'.5402   C97-910173-5

Contents

For Dr. Rod Durkin
America's best-kept secret, with many thanks.

Foreword

by John E. Cockrane, Attorney

Whereas the purchaser (herein called the READER), being of sound mind and character, and notwithstanding physical, emotional, mental or any other problems which render this foreword null and void, agrees not to hold the author(s), publishers, distributors, booksellers or their designated heirs or agents responsible for any injury, perceived or otherwise, whether to the body or mind of the READER, or the body or mind of any person, animal or thing with which the READER comes into contact.

The READER agrees that he/she has sought legal and medical advice before the purchase and/or reading of this book, whenever and wherever it is deemed appropriate to seek such advice under the terms of common law. This foreword is legally binding; void where prohibited by law.

Enjoy!

CHAPTER ONE

You're Not As Good As You Think You Are©

The buck starts here.
—"Sugar" Roy Carboyle,
demotivational psychologist

Introducing Demotivational Psychology

Look at you.

You think you're something special, don't you? You think you're God's gift to the universe. Right? Well, you're wrong, and it's starting to get on everyone's nerves.

The problem is you're *too* good, *too* pumped, *too* motivated. You need to come down a notch. You need to come back to Earth, and then some. You need a crash course in the principles of demotivational psychology.

Why demotivate? For starters, *success can kill you.* It's a medically-proven fact. Well, not actually medically *proven*; but we think if some of those overpaid golf-pros-in-training who pass themselves off as doctors got off their butts and investigated this issue, they'd find that, in fact, success can kill you. For example, we know a man named "Bill." Bill was a "successful" businessman from a "small," midwestern "town." His family asked us—begged us, actually—to keep his identity secret, so suffice to say that "Bill" was owner of Harry's Hardware Haven of Gary, Indiana. One Thursday morning Harry—sorry, "Bill"—was late for work, and sped along Butternut Street in his 1989 Cadillac Seville, when he came to the intersection at 8th Avenue. Perhaps his mind was somewhere else; perhaps he was thinking of his tryst the night before with a hooker named Golda, a liaison which would break his wife's heart were she to learn of it; or perhaps Bill was just in a hurry, knee-deep in that old rat race, pursuing the almighty dollar. Bill took a little less time than he should have at that intersection, and tore off without checking for oncoming traffic. His Cadillac was t-boned by a city bus driven by a moonlighting Presbyterian Minister—who was, apparently, driving under the influence. Harry Yblanski was killed instantly. The ambulance attendants literally scraped that poor man off the pavement, using a shovel purchased—as fate would have it—from Harry's Hardware Haven.

What's the point we're trying to make? We're not sure, but it probably has something to do with *the danger of success*. Think of it. If "Bill" hadn't been a "success" he wouldn't have been able to afford that hooker. If he hadn't been able to afford the hooker, he wouldn't have been racing to work the next morning. If he hadn't been racing to work that morning, he never would have driven his Cadillac, that status symbol of the American Dream, so recklessly. It's a completely true story that shows conclusively: *success can kill you.*

11

Successful People Are Less Happy

You're not convinced? You need another reason to try our demotivational program? How about this. *Successful people are less happy*. It's true. Psychologists have proved it. Okay, a psychologist proved it. Granted, *proved* may be too strong a word. Let's just say that a psychology student we met at a party said that he'd read somewhere that successful people are less happy. It only makes sense. If you were a "success"—in other words, if you had everything you ever wanted or desired—would you be "happy"? If your answer

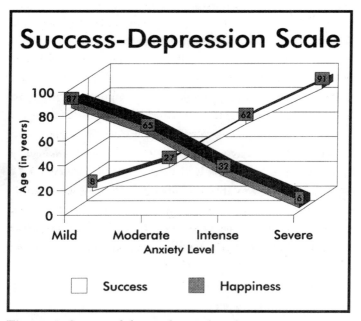

Figure 1: Successful people are less happy.

is "yes," read on. But if you said "no," then this book is definitely for you.

To illustrate the point, here's a story about a man we really knew. It's a poignant tale, which we did not make up simply for the benefit of this book, which illustrates how successful people are less happy. The story concerns a man named Charles. Charles, or "Chuck" as many affectionately called him, was the only son of a poor man and woman, but a fire burned inside him. He was driven to succeed. As a young man, he started working at a small newspaper. In time, he bought the paper and quickly acquired others across the country. Soon he was the most powerful newspaperman in all the country, virtually controlling the free press of America. He ran for Congress, and many said that the President's job was his for the taking.

But Chuck was not happy. In his mad rush for wealth and power, the *trappings of success*, he paid a high price: he had no friends to speak of, only yes-men and lackeys; he had wives and mistresses, but no love; and somewhere along the way, Charles lost his innocence. He died friendless and alone in his mansion on a cold winter's day, clutching a child's toy and muttering a mysterious word over and over again: "Rosebud." We will probably never know what our real life acquaintance meant by his last words, but we are certain of one thing: he was a dink, and all the money, fame and power in the world couldn't change that one simple fact.

How Do I Know Demotivational Psychology Will Work For Me?

Good question. And the simple answer is, you don't. As a wise man once said, there's nothing certain in this world except death and taxis. Or was that death and taxes? We never get it straight.

Anyway, we obviously can't promise that *You're Not as Good as You Think You Are©* will change your life. But we can promise that if you make a sincere effort, and read at least one chapter a day, then in no time at all you'll be finished this book and can move on to something else. And although we can't legally guarantee that this book will change your life, we can offer a personal testimonial which clearly demonstrates the power of demotivational psychology. And who better to offer such an endorsement than "Sugar" Roy Carboyle, the world's foremost expert in the art of demotivation? "Sugar" Roy is the author of such warmly-received-in-certain-circles self-help books as *If You're Networking With Me, Then You Must Be a Loser*; *Buy High, Sell Low*; and the controversial pamphlet *Awakening The Giant In Your Pants: A Self-Growth Guide*. But he wasn't always a relatively obscure author. Once, he was an up-and-coming businessman and entrepreneur, a promising young man on the verge of success. Roy recalls wistfully:

I had it all. A beautiful wife, three or four wonderful children, two cars, a nice house in suburbia, a bread-maker, a large-screen television, one of those beds that goes up and down electronically, a poodle, some duct tape, several large appliances. Did I mention the bread-maker?

14

But one day Roy had a revelation. He was thirty-three years old, and had just been promoted to Area Sales Manager, serving the entire eastern seaboard, for a large telecommunications corporation. He was driving down the Interstate with the CD player blaring Bob Seger's *Greatest Hits* when he saw something that changed his life.

I looked in the rear view mirror and saw for the very first time my own face. I mean, I'd seen it before, but I'd never really looked at it, close up. Real close. So close that my breath steamed up the rear view mirror. I looked beyond the perfect tan and pearl white teeth, past the manicured moustache and $700 hair weave, right through the Ray Bans and rose-coloured contacts into my very own soul. I saw a vast void, and realized that for all my bravado and educated confidence, I was nothing more than a pimple on the butt of humanity. In that moment I experienced what I've come to call a "paradigm collapse"; my perception of the world imploded, as it were, and I felt truly insignificant for the first time in my life. I decided in an instant to forsake my worldly trappings and devote the rest of my life exploring the mediocrity that flourished inside me, and to help others learn to sink deep into their own personal abyss. A moment later, as if a sign from On High, I ran over a badger.

Roy Carboyle spent part of the next ten weeks refining his personal demotivational program then, during lunch at the Red Lobster, printed it neatly on the back of a placemat. This was the blueprint for the easy-to-use demotivational guide you now hold in your hands, a guide which has already helped thousands of people around the world. Okay, maybe "helped" is the wrong word. But it hasn't really hurt anyone, in any permanent physical sense, and now that those lawsuits have been thrown out of court, our low priced legal dream team feel quite comfortable in allowing us to say that there are many fairly positive aspects to this program. It's these aspects that we wish to highlight.

Building a Less Significant You

This book is designed to be as user-friendly as possible. Each chapter focuses on an important aspect of demotivational psychology. By progressing through the book a chapter at a time, you will be reading in a logical and orderly manner. Each chapter provides theory, practical examples from real life, and valuable *Mental Exercises* which will help you hone you skills as you strive to be the very least you can be. Good luck! And we look forward to meeting you at one of our *You're Not as Good as You Think You Are* personal destructional seminars in the near future. Remember our motto: *They're expensive, so you know they must be good.*©

Key Concepts

1. Success can kill you.

2. Successful people are less happy.

3. A fool and his/her money are soon parted.

4. Books are nice, but you just can't beat a good, old-fashioned seminar.

MENTAL EXERCISE 1:
Self-Assessment

Read the following statements. Answer "yes" to the ones that apply to you, and "no" to the ones that don't.

1. Sometimes, I snap at my spouse.

2. Every once in a while, I feel tired or "run down."

3. Occasionally, on a real hot day, I'll drink a couple beers too fast and get a "buzz."

4. Now and then, I feel that a friend, co-worker or family member has "let me down."

5. A couple times, I called into work sick when I wasn't really sick. I just didn't feel like working.

6. More than once I've wondered if my ass was too fat.

7. Quite often when I go to a restaurant, I'll eat too much, and feel mildly uncomfortable for the rest of the evening.

8. I feel intimidated walking the streets of a big city late at night.

9. I'm amazed at how aggressive I become whenever I drive a car.

10. I doubt I'll ever understand even the simplest elements of quantum physics.

If you answered "yes" to any of these statements, then you may have a serious personality or emotional disorder. It is imperative that you read on.

CHAPTER TWO

Chicken Coops for the Soul

"Opportunities are problems waiting to happen."
—Dr. Rod Durkin, Ph.D.,
Psychologist and author of
Recipes for the Good Life

Limiting the Power of Your Imagination

Scientists tell us the average person uses only twenty percent of his or her brain power. If you bought this book, chances are you use even less. What does this tell us about the human condition? Does it mean that with conscious, concerted effort you can unlock the enormous potential hidden in the darkest recesses of your cranium?

No.

What it tells us is that people are, by design, underachievers. The eighty percent of unused brain is Mother Nature's way of keeping us in our place. Most motivational psychologists will try to get you to focus all your energy on expanding your brain power, but this is a waste of effort. If God wanted you to be smarter, you'd be smarter, end of story. In demotivational psychology, the first concept you must accept is that *your brain is your worst enemy*. It's actually shrinking; with every second that ticks by, brain cells are

dying faster than lemmings at high tide. You need to con-
serve your precious brain matter, and to do that, you must
learn to limit the power of your imagination.

Problems Are Everywhere

How do you limit the power of your imagination? The first
step is to recognize that *problems are everywhere*. Most people go through life trying to identify and overcome problems, but this is a big mistake. Perhaps this story will
illustrate our point. It was told to us by Norman "Skippy"
Peale, a distant relative of a famous motivational author.
One day Skippy was walking down the street when a young
man ran up to him and grabbed him by the lapels—which
was quite painful since Skippy wasn't wearing a suit. "I've
got a problem!" the young man screamed.

"You sure do," Skippy replied, and kneed the young man
sharply in the groin.

After regaining his breath, the young man spoke again.
"Please, Mr. Peale. My problems are driving me bananas.
I'm not monkeying around!"

Skippy turned to the young man and said, "Look, I've
got an urgent appointment with my bookie. Before I go see
him, though, I'll show you a place where there are people
with no problems."

"If you show me such a place," said the young man, slyly
avoiding a copyright violation, "I'll gnaw off my left arm to
get in there."

A smile slowly swept across Skippy's face. "Whatever,"

he said, with a rather evil sounding laugh. "But you might not like what you see when you get there." He laughed again. "Come on, it's only a few blocks away."

Skippy and the young man walked to Shady Acres, a nearby cemetery. Skippy pointed to the graveyard and said: "Look. There's a whole bunch of people here, and I don't hear any of them complaining."

The young man fell silent.

"Get it? They're dead, so they don't have any problems! So, do you still want to join them?" Skippy was doubled over with laughter; tears welled in his eyes, he was laughing so hard.

The young man's face flushed. "You tricked me," he said. There was more than a hint of menace in his tone.

"I was only trying to make a point. . . ."

"You lied to me. No one lies to me and gets away with it."

And then all hell broke loose. You see, the young man was a psychopath. Skippy was lucky to get away with a mild concussion, three cracked ribs and a broken wrist. And what does this story tell us? Simply put, problems are everywhere. And quite often, when we try to overcome one problem, we wind up, like Skippy, in a much bigger pickle.

So, Where Is This All Leading?

Another good question. You see, most people are essentially optimistic, oblivious to the fact that defeat and death lurk behind every door and every smiling face. It takes a colossal amount of imagination—pure mental energy—to

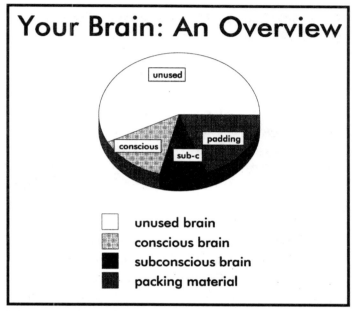

Figure 2: Brain Matrix

maintain this illusion, and consequently, the natural process of brain disintegration is significantly enhanced.

In order to overcome this unhealthy belief system, you need to undergo a *paradigm collapse*. You must completely destroy your current mode of thinking.

But let's not get ahead of ourselves.

First, you have to understand that each person creates his or her own perception of the world. In fact, it's possible for two people to witness the exact same event, but walk away with completely different perceptions. Anyone who's ever had casual sex can attest to this. Or here's a more potent example, from an actual true-life experience of

23

"Sugar" Roy Carboyle, inventor of demotivational psychology and co-author of *You're Not as Good as You Think You Are©*:

When I was at Harvard University, attending a non-credit seminar in calligraphy, I had an experience that I'll never forget. Fortunately, the goat's owner was fairly liberal-minded. I also remember the time that the seminar leader conducted a little exercise that demonstrated the transience of perception. One day, he brought a paper bag to class and set it on his desk. Slowly, he opened the bag to reveal a can of beer. But this was no ordinary can of beer. This was a can of "lite" beer. The instructor opened the can and took a swig. He smacked his lips, then guzzled half the can. "Ahhh," he groaned with satisfaction. "More taste!"

At that moment, one of the female students sitting near the front of the class grabbed the can and guzzled the remaining beer. "Mmmm," she said wistfully. "Less filling!"

The teacher looked at the student with alarm. "More taste!"

"Less filling!" the student replied, jumping to her feet.

It looked like they would come to blows. But fortunately, the Dean appeared at that moment with a case of ice cold beer under each arm. "Hold your horses," he sang in such a friendly tone that all the tension in the room instantly evaporated. "You're both right! Lite beer has more taste and is less filling." With those words, the Dean lay the cases of beer on the desk, ripped a box open, and popped a can of the nut-brown nectar. The Dean took a deep, long drink, then wiped his lips on his jacket sleeve. "No matter how you slice it," he said wisely, "that's one damn fine drink!"

The point the Dean was making was that we assume when we

experience an event, everyone else experiences it in the exact same way. But as this exercise proved, perception is a highly personal thing. More taste? Less filling? Both teacher and student were right.

And at the same time, both were wrong.

As "Sugar" Roy Carboyle's rambling parable illustrates, perception is really a matter of an individual's point of view; you might even say that one's point of view *dictates* one's perception of events. Or to put it another way, the point of view, which is yours, has a profound impact on the way you perceive things that happen in the everyday real world. It's a small point really, but we can't stress it too much. We suggest you just accept it, then you will be on your way to unleashing the pathetic nobody lurking inside the shallowest depths of your soul. You might call it a *wrong* step in the *right* direction.

On the other hand, you might not.

Key Concepts

1. Scientists tell us the average person uses only twenty percent of his or her brain power. This is nature's way of keeping us in our place.

2. Your brain is your worst enemy.

3. Perception is in the eye of the beholder, figuratively speaking.

4. Lite beer: more taste *and* less filling.

MENTAL EXERCISE 2:
From Winner to Wiener

Most of us go through life striving to be winners, keeping the wiener inside us at bay. We want to be "successful," forgetting that successful people are born that way. It's a matter of simple genetics, and the bitter truth is, if you're not a winner now, you're never going to be one. There are a lot of "good" reasons for not succeeding; here are just a few. Check this list and see if you can't find at least three good reasons which prove, beyond a reasonable doubt, that you are destined to remain forever a loser.

1. I'm too ugly.

2. I'm not ugly enough.

3. I'm too fat.

4. I'm not fat enough.

5. I have a peculiar body odour.

6. My body odour is not peculiar enough.

7. I have a voice in my head, urging me to kill people.

8. I have a voice in my head urging me not to kill people.

9. I belong to an ethnic, sexual, physical, religious, mental, intellectual or political minority group.

10. I don't belong to an ethnic, sexual, physical, religious, mental, intellectual or political minority group but I want people to feel sorry for me anyway.

11. I have not mastered Texas line dancing.

12. I have mastered Texas line dancing.

13. I don't have my own network television show.

14. I do have my own network television show, but it's on Fox.

15. My ass is too big.

CHAPTER THREE

The Power
of
Negative Thinking

What lies before us and what lies behind us
are tiny matters compared to what lies in our way.
—Kevin Gudgeon, co-author's brother

The ABC of Demotivational Psychology

Always be critical.

It's the ABC of demotivational psychology. The critical person is always ready for any eventuality, always on guard to snatch defeat from the jaws of victory. It's what we call *the power of negative thinking*, and it can change your life.

To fully understand the power of negative thinking we first need to review some basic psychological concepts—the hard core, leading edge scientific principles that form the foundation of any serious study of the human mind.

Basic Concepts in Psychology

I. Central Concepts

Behaviourism: The study of how organisms learn. The most famous of the behaviourists is B.F. (Big Friendly) Skinner. Skinner asserts that all learning is the result of conditioned responses (CR) to stimuli (S). His most famous book, *Dating The Hard Way*, explores this theory of learned behaviour, and culminates in Skinner's now famous conclusion: the influence of conditioned responses (CS) is directly proportional to the size of the grant being pursued (GBP). See: Skinner's Box.

Developmentalism: The study of qualitative changes in the course of the human lifespan. The pioneer in this field is Swiss psychologist Jean (The Big Cheese) Piaget. Piaget spent his life watching children arrange blocks, pour water from one container to another and play tag, until one day he cried, "Okay, I give! Can I do something useful now?" Piaget was a close friend of Einstein, and often borrowed the physicist's lawnmower for months on end. See: Piaget's Box.

Psychoanalysis: The grandparent of modern psychiatry. The founder of psychoanalysis is Sigmund Freud. Freud conceived of the human mind as a closed system, composed of the unconscious "id," the "super ego" (what Freud termed "Humanity's maiden aunt"), and the "ego" (as in, "Let go of my ego"). Many of the concepts introduced by Freud have gained popular use (See: Glossary). However, the recently discovered *Lost Writings of Sigmund Freud* have turned the psychoanalytic world on its ear. In this book, Freud rejects his earlier model to offer an open- ended psyche, "much like a corporate tax return." Instead of "id" and "ego," Freud suggests the psyche is ruled by "some fat guy called Pepé" and the cast of an all-male musical revue, *Viking For Hire!*

II. Other Important Influences

Carl Jung: Jung, a student of Freud, spent his life correcting people who mispronounced his last name ("Dat's Yung," he'd say. "Yung! Just like Robert Yung on *Father Knows Best*"). Jung introduced the concept of introvert/extrovert to popular culture, although he was never clear if this should be taken seriously. Jung broke with Freud, calling him "old, and somewhat German." Jung grew reclusive and, in the end, believed he would one day be reincarnated as Shirley MacLaine.

Pavlov: A Russian researcher whose studies on dog saliva were instrumental in laying the groundwork for Behaviourism (See above). Later, Pavlov moved from dog saliva to the study of hairballs, kitty litter and, eventually, toddlers' vomit.

Erik Erikson (a.k.a. Eric Ericson, Erik the Red, Eric the Greek and Milly Hamilton): Another student of Freud. Erikson is best known for his characterization of the basic issues in human development:
  1. Trust vs. Mistrust
  2. Autonomy vs. Self-Doubt

3. Shame vs. Everything
4. Leafs vs. Habs
5. Cat vs. Dog
6. Man vs. Woman
7. Lawyer vs. Lawyer

Masters and Johnson: American sex researchers who accidentally discovered the female orgasm while double dating.

III. Glossary of Terms

Oedipus Complex: Freudian concept, in which the male child unconsciously longs to murder his father and marry his mother. If issue not resolved during childhood, may lead to such deviant behaviour as shoplifting or membership in the Reform Party.

Skinner's Box: Small maze designed by B.F. Skinner. Its purpose was to give anti-social graduate students an excuse to work weekends.

Penis Envy: Another Freudian concept, indicating the woman's unconscious desire to possess a penis (or, at least, one belonging to someone other than her husband).

Piaget's Box: Piaget built a box of his own, in the belief it would make him "better known, like Skinner."

Dental Floss: Waxed or unwaxed, used to clean teeth and stimulate gums. Not generally regarded as a psychological term, but gaining favour in some circles.

Gestalt: 1. A branch of psychology which stresses the whole pattern rather than a single part. 2. The sound of a sneeze.

Freud's Box: On seeing Skinner's and Piaget's boxes, Freud declared: "I must have one longer and thicker than all the others."

But What Does This Really Tell Us About the Human Mind?

Not much. But it may come in handy at your next cocktail party. So maybe we should just stick to the basics. Scientists tell us that the human brain is actually made up of two separate but interdependent parts called the *conscious* and the *subconscious*. These are actual compartments in the brain—or, as neurologists call it, the "think bone"—where all thought processes take place. Of course, no one has

$$(\text{Conscious} \rightarrow \odot \leftarrow \text{Subconscious}) \leq \mathbf{DP}_{\circledR}$$

Figure 3: Your brain vs. a registered trademark.

actually seen these two compartments, but you can take our word for it, they exist.

The conscious and subconscious are mortal enemies. Kind of like Superman and Lex Luthor. Or, to be more scientific, the Good and Bad Kirks in that *Star Trek* episode. The conscious mind makes all the decisions, plans a sensible course for our lives; it is the house of virtue, intellect, compassion and reason. The subconscious undermines the conscious at every turn; it waits in the mire for the conscious mind to pass, then it leaps out and attacks. The subconscious is home, like some dark Frankenstein castle, to all our base desires and impulses.

The problem is that most of us live almost exclusively in the "conscious" house, building walls and fences to keep our lousy subconscious neighbours at bay. Our conscious mind trains itself to overlook the despair and pure animal ferocity that is the human condition, and we pass our days wearing mental blinders.

But the good news is that with a little effort we can program our conscious minds to think negatively. The trick is to remember our demotivational ABC: *always be critical*. We must train our minds to create and reinforce a negative perception of the world. It's not an easy job, and chances are you'll never be able to completely master it. But thanks to our patent-pending system of *Daily Defirmations*®, your task just got a whole lot easier.

What are defirmations? Simply put, they are *negative self-statements that reinforce a defeatist self-image or world view*. They were developed by "Sugar" Roy Carboyle, a former telephone solicitor and now the foremost demotivational psychologist in the world. Roy, who spends much of his time these days helping people just like you lead unrewarding and less fulfilling lives, says that his program of *Daily Defirmations®* is both a "powerful tool" and "registered trade name, protected by international copyright law."

Defirming Yourself

The art of defirmation is both simple and mysterious; it's most effective on simple-minded people like you, and it's a mystery how anyone will fall for this crap. Having said that, there are some steps you can take to put yourself in the right frame of mind to benefit fully from defirmations.

Step 1. Stand.
This will bring your consciousness to its fullest state of awareness. This is a medical fact, and we're not just making it up.

Step 2. Bark.
That's right. Bark like the dog you are. Barking puts our subconscious into a state of submissiveness, causing it to become "best friend" to the dominant, conscious "master." There are a lot of complicated scientific reasons for this, but we don't need to go into them. Again, just take our word for it.

Step 3. Poke yourself.
Take the middle finger of your left hand and extend it fully. Poke yourself vigorously and repeatedly in the face, throat

or chest. This engages your sense of touch. Your middle finger is scientifically proven to be way more sensitive than any other part of your body, even that special little place you-know-where that you sometimes secretly like to play with when no one's looking. Keep poking yourself until it hurts, until you become angry and irritated with yourself.

Step 4. Shout.
Once you've got yourself good and mad, shout one of the sample defirmations at yourself in a stern voice. Don't pussyfoot around. The verbal abuse you heap on yourself will have no value if you don't really mean it!

Following are a few sample defirmations—and don't forget to watch for *"Sugar" Roy Carboyle's Daily Defirmations®*, a full year's worth of negative self-statements which will soon be available in book, tape, video, CD-ROM, braille and Morse code.

Poke yourself and shout: "I suck. I really, really suck!"
Poke yourself and shout: "I am a bad person!"
Poke yourself and shout: "I do not deserve to be a success!"
Poke yourself and shout: "I will never find that special someone!"
Poke yourself and shout: "I am the boil on the ass of humanity!"
Poke yourself and shout: "My taste in clothes leaves a lot to be desired!"
Poke yourself and shout: "I have bad breath!"
Poke yourself and shout: "I am unattractive in many ways!"

Poke yourself and shout: "My teeth are crooked and yellow!"

Poke yourself and shout: "My posture is poor!"

Poke yourself and shout: "My unusual behaviour makes people nervous!"

Poke yourself and shout: "My head is disproportionate to my body!"

Poke yourself and shout: "That growth on my arm is probably cancerous!"

Poke yourself and shout: "If I don't stop poking myself I'm going to go mental!"

Key Concepts

1. Always be critical. It's the ABC of demotivational psychology.

2. The human brain is actually made up of two separate but interdependent parts called the *conscious* and the *subconscious*; they are mortal enemies.

3. We must train our mind to create and reinforce a negative perception of the world.

4. Defirmations are negative self-statements, protected by international copyright law.

MENTAL EXERCISE 3:
The Inexpensive Art of Self-Touch

Practice makes perfect, even in demotivational psychology, so it is important that you take the time to practice your daily defirmations. The shower is an excellent place for you to work; quiet and solitary, it's an ideal environment for you to get to know yourself a little better.

Go to your bathroom and slowly undress yourself. Dim the lights a little, if that makes you feel more relaxed. Turn on the water and fix yourself a nice, warm shower. Step into the shower stall. Ooops! It's too cold.

That's better.

Now, touch yourself. Touch yourself and say: "I've been very, very naughty."

You *have* been naughty. You deserve a spanking.

Lather up your hand with soap and spank your buttocks firmly but not too hard. Strike it again, more forcefully. Now harder. Does it hurt? No? You've been a very naughty person and must be properly punished. Spank yourself harder! Did that hurt? Good.

Now, rub soap all over your naked, wet body. Touch yourself again. You know where. That special secret place that—mmmmm—feels so good. That's right, touch yourself harder and faster and . . .

* * *

If you'd like to finish this Mental Exercise, call 1-900-YOU-SUCK. Our sexy "therapists" are waiting to "defirm" you. Only $2.99/minute. Must be over 18. Operators are standing by.

CHAPTER FOUR

Giant Steps, Backwards

You can be anything you want,
as long as you don't want a lot.
—Dr. Al "Fingers" Olson, proctologist

The Art of Setting Self-Defeating Goals

A woman we know—let's call her "Dorothy"—had a dilemma. Dorothy believed that her life was lacking, but she couldn't put her finger on the exact problem. So Dorothy decided to go on a trip, a kind of mythical voyage of self-discovery. She escaped her dreary, black and white world, the "here and now," and travelled to a magical, technicolour world where everything seemed possible. It was a land where animals talked, where the roads were literally paved with gold, a land of "witches" overseen by an aging, benevolent "wizard."

No, Dorothy wasn't on acid. But she had been struck on the head during a tornado, and the place she visited, which she called "Oz," was in fact a distant world in her imagination. Eventually, Dorothy came to her senses and woke up from her dreamland to discover that her imaginary wanderings were all for naught. She was right back where she had started: in a dingy hovel, on some godforsaken dirt farm in the middle of nowhere, surrounded by a bunch of fading vaudeville hams. It's a true story, told to us in strictest confidence by one of our closest and dearest friends, and it illustrates the value of *goal-setting* in everyday life. Dorothy didn't know where she was going because she didn't know where she wanted to end up. And along the way, as she headed toward this uncertain destination, the end eventually became the means, or simply put, the end became the end in and unto itself.

Perhaps we're not making ourselves clear.

Behavioural psychologists tell us that any human activity needs direction and focus in order to be successful. Of course, why should we listen to a bunch of overpaid, under-socialized eggheads? Suffice to say that goals in general are important, and specifically, the art of setting self-defeating goals is essential to demotivational psychology. It reiterates our earlier point that people are essentially optimistic, believing that, with a little bit of elbow grease, everything will turn out just fine. When they go to bed at night, it never occurs to them that the sun might not rise the next day. Therefore, they spend their lives making plans—shopping lists, business itineraries, dinner engagements, hair appointments—a continuous cycle of goal-attainment which provides them with the illusion of achievement. In order to receive the full benefit of demotivational psychology, you must break this delusional cycle and cultivate the art of self-defeating goals.

Aren't You Starting to Repeat Yourself?

There are three basic self-defeating goal strategies: *Fat Chance Goals*; *Small Potato Goals*; and *Goal Overload*. *Fat Chance Goals* are unrealistic ones, which reinforce failure, while *Small Potato Goals* are self-limiting, thus ensuring your continued mediocrity. *Goal Overload* is a method of clustering a number of smaller goals until they reach an unmanageable proportion. Let's look at each of these important strategies in more detail.

Fat Chance Goals: Choose a goal. Let's say you decide that within the next three months, you are going to become a starting quarterback in the National Football League. You are going to work hard, harder than you've ever worked in your life. You are going to hire a fitness trainer, a dietician, a physiotherapist, and a former pro quarterback as your personal consultant. You will sink your life savings into this one crazy scheme, but dammit, for once in your life you've finally decided to go for broke. People will laugh at you; of course they will. But that won't deter you. You will keep at it, honing your skills further and spending more and more of your hard-earned money on a chance for your moment in the limelight. And through it all, one simple thought will keep you focused: *you haven't got a hope in hell*. At the end of three months, you will be a little fitter—maybe—and a lot poorer. You will hate yourself for the time and resources that you have so foolishly squandered. You will, once again, have to resign yourself to the fact that you are another faceless, nameless schlep, limping your way to obscurity.

Congratulations. You've just had your first taste of what

demotivational psychologists call *fat chance goal-setting*. It's perfectly designed for baby boomers who were brought up on the unrealistic belief that they could do anything as long as they set their minds to it. The first step in fat chance goal-setting is to select an objective that you have no chance of achieving. Maybe you're going to become the first accountant on the moon. Perhaps you're going to make your way into the *Guinness Book of World Records* by swallowing a 1977 Ford Pinto, piece by piece. Or perhaps you want to set your sights on circumnavigating the globe, on a bicycle made entirely of Graham crackers. It doesn't matter what goal you set, as long as it is completely unreal-

Figure 4: The Goals Matrix.

istic—for some of you, it could be as simple as reading a book on calculus.

The second step is to established a time frame. It should be short enough to maintain your interest, yet long enough to squeeze every ounce of misery out of your ultimate failure. We suggest one to three months, with this rule of thumb: the more unrealistic your goal, the less time you should devote to it.

The third and most important step is that you tell as many people as possible about your goal. When they scoff at you or try to talk you out of it, cultivate an air of deep indignation; how dare they question your iron will? Remember: the more people you tell, the more embarrassed you will be when you finally give up on your lofty ambition.

Small Potato Goals: Imagine that the world is your oyster, but unfortunately, you're allergic to seafood. Therefore, you have to settle for something second best. And why not? That's all you deserve. This is the kind of thinking that powers the small potato self-limiting goal strategy. By setting your sights low on easily obtainable goals, you guarantee that you'll be a chronic underachiever who never lives up to his or her potential. It's a simple strategy which you can apply to any aspect of your life. At work, for example, strive for a demotion. In the area of relationships, you could try to piss off an average of one friend or family member per month. When it comes to your health, you could work toward packing on another fifteen pounds.

Goal Overload: Imagine you have the afternoon off and all you want to do is go to the bank. Simple. In fact, too simple.

So you decide to go to the library as well, to drop off those overdue books, and pop into the pet store to buy some kitty litter. Then of course, you remember that the pet store is near the hair salon, so you could get your hair done as well, and why not drop in on your aunt Miranda, even though she's a disagreeable old so-and-so, but you'll be in the neighbourhood. . . .

Eventually, you'll have added enough side trips that your original goal—going to the bank—gets lost in the shuffle. This is the essence of Goal Overload. It's something we all do unconsciously, but in demotivational psychology, we work to develop this into a conscious strategy. The idea is

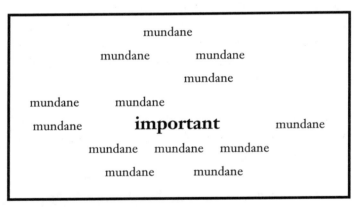

Figure 5: Goal Overload.

to cluster a large number of goals together in a limited time period. It's most effective when you cluster a large group of mundane goals around an important one. The beauty of this strategy is that you can constantly add to your goal cluster until you create a ongoing sense of helplessness, a self-perpetuating cycle of failure.

It's hard to believe that these three simple goal-setting strategies could change your life, but it's true. They were designed by Dr.* "Sugar" Roy Carboyle, the world's foremost authority on demotivational psychology, as well as inventor of the Calf Cruncher**, a patented home exercise machine which helps you sculpt gargantuan, manly calf muscles in less than a month. According to Carboyle, a demotivational program without self- defeating goals is, quite literally, like a "manly person without disproportionately enormous calf muscles." So confident is Carboyle in the power of this goal-setting system, that he's prepared to offer a money-back guarantee to anyone who isn't completely satisfied with this demotivational system. However, his lawyers have advised against this, so you're on your own.

---

*Of Mixology. Eds.
**Not to be confused with the portable home rendering machine of the same name. Eds.

Key Concepts

1. Human activity needs direction and focus in order to be successful.

2. The art of setting self-defeating goals is essential to demotivational psychology.

3. There are three basic kinds of self-defeating goal strategies: *Fat Chance Goals*, *Small Potato Goals*, and *Goal Overload*.

4. You can't buy happiness, but you can buy manly calf muscles.

MENTAL EXERCISE 4:

Practice What We Preach

Part A: Circle the correct response in the exercises below.

1. Identify *Fat Chance Goals* from the following list:
   a) I am going to become a brain surgeon.
   b) I am going to create a race of supermen and women who will worship me as their leader.
   c) I am going to write a best-selling demotivational guide.

2. Select an appropriate time frame to achieve a *Fat Chance Goal*:
   a) One month.
   b) Six to eight weeks, excluding weekends.
   c) Three hours, tops, if I really work at it.

3. Identify the most effective *Small Potato Goal* from the following list:
   a) I will get a job at a fast food restaurant.
   b) I will rob a fast food restaurant.
   c) I will eat at every fast food restaurant in town.

Part B: Create a Goal Overload cluster from the following list.

a) Pick up laundry.

b) Rotate tires.

c) Return videos.

d) Fix button on yellow shirt.

e) Go to grandpa's funeral.

f) Pay gas bill.

g) Reprogram car stereo.

h) Make "To Do" list.

ANSWERS

Part A: 1-a,b; 2-a,b; 3-c.

Part B:

Rotate tires

Pick up laundry   Return videos

Wash car   Go to grandpa's funeral   pay gas bill

Fix buttons on shirt   Reprogram car stereo

Make 'To Do' List

CHAPTER FIVE

Dare to Whine!

Pithy quotations at the start of a chapter are an easy way
to make you seem smarter than you really are.
—Anthony "Lips" Nelson,
unemployed corporate executive

Understanding the Win/Whine Paradigm

By now you've acquired all the basic skills you need to success-
fully demotivate, and you've probably begun to feel less significant, less effective and, in the case of presidential
candidates, less likely to commit an indictable offense. But
your hard work will be wasted if you don't change your basic
philosophy for dealing with the world. Perhaps this simple
story will illustrate our point. It comes from the mouth of our
own "Sugar" Roy Carboyle, whose first self-help book *Beauty
Secrets of Attila the Hun* was an international bestseller, setting
the stage for his protracted and mediocre literary career:

*Once, the night manager of a medium-sized grocery store asked
me for help. His name was Morton, and he was concerned about
dissension among his staff.*

*"They just can't seem to get along, Roy," Morton said, confi-
dently using my first name in order to add an air of authenticity*

to the anecdote. "They're always at each other's throats, Roy, and I don't know what to do."

To make a long story short, I agreed to help Morton. All I asked for in return was a flat fee plus a retainer and modest per diem. After he met with my lawyers and signed several waivers, I visited him in his store. I was amazed to see that, while he preached co-operation, Morton subtly encouraged competition among his staff. For example, he offered cash bonuses to employees who met or exceeded sales targets. More divisive was his habit of talking behind his employees' backs. Then of course, there were the mandatory, winner-take-all bare-knuckle boxing matches every Friday night in the produce department.

I explained to Morton that, as unintentional as it was, he had turned the workplace into a "culture of competition." Under my direction, Morton put an end to the cash bonuses, took a course in effective communication so he could talk openly and honestly with his staff, and stopped the Friday night fight-fests in the produce department (he moved them to the deli, a larger venue that could accommodate many more spectators).

Despite my best efforts, the entire staff quit en masse the following week, which just goes to show that there's just no pleasing some people.

Isn't That Just Another One of Your Pointless Parables?

No. The point is that human behaviour is unpredictable. No matter how much money we shell out to the so-called "experts," no one can guarantee how an individual will react in a given set of circumstances. That's what makes the world such an interesting place, and why we make people like Morton sign waivers. Having said all this, we do know that human behaviour is relatively predictable. For example, most people will respond to you on the basis of your own style of interpersonal communication. In Morton's case, he opted for a confrontational style, what we call the *Win/Lose Approach*. But this is just one of the strategies that people use to interrelate. Psychologists—and other professionals with access to a thesaurus—call these strategies *paradigms*. Extensive scientific research has revealed that there are exactly eleven basic paradigms of human interaction. No more, no less.

Exactly eleven.

Are There Really Only Eleven "Paradigms" of Human Interaction?

Yes. And here they are, in no particular order:

1. Win/Win.
2. Lose/Win.
3. Lose/Lose.
4. Win/Lose.
5. Win/Lose/Draw.
6. Win/Win/Lose/Win/Lose.
7. Win/Lose/Lose/Lose/Win/Lose/Lose/Win.
8. Win/Lose/Lose/Lose/Lose/Win a little/
   Lose/Lose big.

9. Win some/Lose some.
10. Winsome/Lonesome.
11. Win/Whine.

While all these paradigms have their place, we want to focus on the last one. *Win/Whine* is not just a general rule

The Win/Lose/Whine Matrix			
	Win	**Lose**	**Whine**
Win	Win/Win	Win/Lose	Win/Whine
Lose	Lose/Win	Lose/Lose	Lose/Whine
Whine	Whine/Win	Whine/Lose	Whine/Whine

Figure 6: The Win/Whine Paradigm Matrix.

of behaviour; it constitutes an entire philosophy of life. As profound and idiomatic as metaphysics, and at the same time as moving, although less acerbic, as logical positivism, the *Win/Whine Paradigm* ranks among the major intellectual breakthroughs of the 20th century—as long as you don't count things like the discovery of penicillin, Neil Armstrong's moonwalk, or Einstein's Theory of Relativity.

The *Win/Whine Paradigm* is a foolproof method to get others to reinforce your new-found, negative self-image. Nobody likes a whiner, and in particular, nobody likes a winner who whines. By using the *Win/Whine* strategy —bending every rule of common decency in order to gain the upper hand in a situation, then finding reasons to complain about your victory—you are sure to earn the disdain of everyone you meet. By having people dislike you on sight, and by training them to cringe at the very sound of your footsteps, you not only alter their perception of you, but your own perception of yourself.

How exactly does the *Win/Whine Paradigm* work? Well, why don't you ask us, and maybe we'll explain it to you?

All Right. How Exactly Does the Win/Whine Paradigm Work?

That wasn't very sincere. Try one more time.

Please, Please, Please Explain How the Win/Whine Paradigm Works!

That's better. Basically, *Win/Whine* is a four-step process. First, *define* the issue. This is the problem evaluation phase, when you first recognize that there is a potential confrontation in the offing. Next, *refine* the problem. Clarify some of the finer points of the issue or simply make some inflammatory comment. Third, *confine* the issue. In other words, take control of the situation by using such aggressive tactics as an irrational demand or a hurtful barb. Finally, *opine* the issue. Change your role from victor to victim.

The *Win/Whine Paradigm* might sound complicated, but isn't that just the way it goes with all great ideas? We're talking about major intellectual breakthroughs of the century here; did you really think you'd pick it up the first time through? In any case, here are a few examples to show you how to put the *Win/Whine Paradigm* into practice. We've finished the first one for you; in the others, complete the sentence by circling the most appropriate response.

Example 1: Arguing with spouse

Define: "So you think *I'm* lazy and stupid, do you?"

Refine: "Well, I think *you're* lazy and stupid!"

Confine: "In fact, I think you're twice as lazy and stupid as me."

Opine: "Now you're mad at me?! I guess I just can't win!"

Example 2: Demeaning an employee

Define: "I told you that I needed those orders processed by 5:00."

Refine: "I think *you're* _____ and _____."
(a slow worker/lazy) (a dilly-dallier/stupid)

Confine: "I have no choice but to _____ you."
(inappropriately touch/fire)

Opine: "Now you're mad at me?! I guess I just can't _____." (offer you a raise/win)

Example 3: Humiliating a waiter

Define: "I asked for a rare steak; this steak is medium rare."

Refine: "I think *you're* _____ and _____."
(a person who doesn't listen well/lazy; perhaps

suffering from some kind of attention disorder
/stupid)

Confine: "Get me the owner, I'll have your _____!"
(outfit/job)

Opine: "Now you're mad at me?! I guess I just can't
_____."(withhold your tip/win)

Take a few moments to think up some examples of your own, and see how easy it is to turn your winning ways into whining ways.

Key Concepts

1. There are exactly eleven paradigms of human interaction, no more, no less. So stop worrying already.

2. There's a fine line between winning and whining.

3. There's no excuse, and no replacement, for bad manners.

MENTAL EXERCISE 5:
The More Than Half-Way Through Review

1. Lite beer. More taste? Less filling? Discuss.

2. Explain, in detail, why you will never amount to a hill of beans.

3. In retrospect, who really won the race: the tortoise or the hare? Discuss.

4. Write an essay on one of the following topics:
    a) Tony Orlando and his impact on popular music today.
    b) Al Gore: Man on a mission.
    c) Aspects of irony in the films of Don Knotts.
    d) Canada: Belgium of the Americas?

5. Describe, in painful detail, your least attractive physical feature.

6. Make a list of your ten least appealing personal qualities. Show five friends the list. Solicit their comments, corrections, and additions.

CHAPTER SIX

The Roads Not Taken

A journey of a single step starts with a thousand excuses.
—Barbara Stewart, former Toastmaster

The Hidden Wisdom in Indecision
and Procrastination

Like all things, wisdom is relative. It's possible for a very stupid person to be very wise in his or her own way. Similarly, it's possible for a very wise person to be profoundly stupid, especially when it comes to personal grooming habits. And just as there is a particular kind of wisdom that befits a philosopher more than a dogcatcher—and, for that matter, a particular wisdom that befits a dogcatcher more than a dental hygienist—there is a unique wisdom best-suited to the demotivated person.

To fully appreciate the transient nature of wisdom, consider this famous story of the great King Solomon. He was renowned throughout the Holy Land as a man of tremendous wisdom. His Code of Ethics served as the basis for the first democratic government. His poems, the Psalms, are admired to this day for their subtle beauty. He is the legendary inventor of kielbasa, a spicy hot snack sausage. And it was through his research in folk medicine that the first childproof bottle was developed. Here is an anecdote which illustrates his profound wisdom, as recorded by the gnostic scholar Horace the Incontinent:

Once, the High Priest Akumembar brought forth two women and a baby. Each woman claimed the infant boy as her own.

"He has my eyes," the first woman said. "Any fool can see that!"

Indeed, the first woman did have raven eyes, like the babe, and was singular in her beauty.

"Oh come on! Look at his nose." The second woman—who, by coincidence, was also singular in her beauty—held the baby up to her face. "See? Has there ever been a mother and child with more similar noses? It even peaks up at the end, just like mine."

"You lying witch!" shouted the first woman.

The two began to tug at the child, one on each arm, until the guards separated them.

The priests were puzzled. How could anyone tell which woman was honest, and which was lying? Solomon summoned the babe to be brought forth to him. A guard laid the infant on a pillow at the king's feet. "Bring me one of those sharp, pointy things with a curve," Solomon declared.

"A scimitar?" the Sergeant-At-Arms asked.

"Yes, that's the thing. Bring me a, um, schmintler!"

Solomon stood above the child, scimitar in hand, and thus addressed the throng.

"Since both of you claim equal share of the child, an equal share you shall have. I shall cleft the babe in two with this, um, big sword, and present half to each of you."

The priests looked at one another and nodded their heads. He was indeed a wise and wonderful man.

Solomon raised his sword. "On the count of three. One. Two—"

"Stop!" the raven-eyed woman cried.

Solomon lowered the sword, and cast a knowing glance to the assembled priests.

"Would I get the top half or the bottom half?" she asked.

"Neither top nor bottom; I said I was going to cleft him down the middle, two roughly symmetrical pieces."

"What's that mean, 'roughly symmetrical'?"

"Two pieces of approximately the same size and shape."

The raven-eyed woman nodded her head. The king proceeded.

"One. Two. Two and a half. I'm really just about to say three. Thhhhhhhh. Don't try to stop me. Thrrrr—"

"Hang on!" the peak-nosed woman screamed.

Again Solomon lowered his sword. "I want the right half; how do I know she won't get it?" she snarled at her adversary.

"We'll, um, draw straws. Short straw gets first pick. All right? One. Two. This time I'm serious. Thrrrrr—" the King lowered his sword. "I'm really going to cut him. Crunch! Right down the middle."

The two women nodded, and waited for the wise king to continue.

"We can't just stick him back together later, you know."

The women stared blankly.

"Oh dammit! One. Two. Three." The sword came down and cut with a single, effortless stroke.

"There," the king said. "Are you happy?"

At that moment a third woman ran into the royal chamber. "Oh my God!" she screamed. "What have you done to my baby? He's cleft in two!"

Thinking quickly, the wise king hid the scimitar behind his back. "What baby?" he asked, innocently.

"Don't give me that crap! You've cut him in half with your stupid sabre."

"It's not a sabre. For your information a sabre is a heavy, one-edged cavalry sword, with a thick-back blade, often curved. This is a scmermermermer." Solomon faded into a murmur.

Akumembar could no longer contain himself. He began to chuckle most resolutely.

"What's the big joke, pal?"

"Does His Majesty know what day it is today?" Akumembar asked, wiping a mirthful tear from his eye.

"Of course I know what day it is, I'm not a complete fool. It's Monday."

"No my Lord, I mean: do you know what the date is?"

"Why yes it is the first day of April, in the 1098th year according to the old calendar—." Suddenly Solomon understood. A smile crossed his face.

"April Fool!" the priests cried in unison, and broke into a chorus of laughter.

"I wish I had a drawing of your face when that woman ran in looking for her baby!" Akumembar said, slapping his knee.

"Well, I've got to admit, you guys had me hook, line and sinker. But tell me, who are these women?"

"They're professional actresses from Damascus; we had them couriered in by camel today."

"And the babe?"

"A papyrus replica, sire."

"Clever indeed! Splendid joke, gentlemen! And you know, there's a lesson here for all of us." The great king appeared quite thoughtful. "Everyone," he said wisely, "everyone is better off if they can only learn to laugh at themselves."

The learned priests nodded, then quietly reflected for a moment. And that evening, they all had a good laugh when they found live scorpions in their bed clothes. And with their dying chortles another valuable lesson came to mind.

Never fuck with a king.

That's Great for a High Priest, but What About Me?

The wisdom of Solomon is universal. But what about the wisdom of the demotivated person? Is there a particular kind of wisdom specific to his or her situation? The answer is "Yes"—and thank goodness for that, or this would be an unusually short chapter!

The key to wisdom is not in where you find it but where you look for it. Bakers find wisdom in bread. Farmers find wisdom in fields. Dentists find wisdom in teeth. And where do demotivational psychologists find wisdom? According to our own "Sugar" Roy Carboyle—the world's foremost demotivational psychologist, and former president of the Grover Cleveland High School Audio-Visual Club—wisdom can be found through contemplation of the "dual virtues" of *indecision* and *procrastination*. According to Carboyle, "A divided mind is unconquerable, deferral can never be defeated."

Why search for profound meaning within indecision and procrastination? Simply put, wasted effort and inaction are your best friends. It's impossible to be motivated when you can't even decide which video to rent. And no one has yet to be elected President of the United States by declaring, "What the heck, I can wait another four years." So don't delay: divide and defer today!

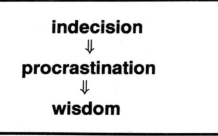

Figure 7: The Wisdom Flowchart.

Key Concepts

1. All things are relative, and conversely, all relatives are things.

2. Wisdom, like beauty or a sense of humour, is in the eye of the beholder.

3. Always put off today what you can do tomorrow.

MENTAL EXERCISE 6:

Be a Power Procrastinator!*

---

* Note: Mental Exercise 6 not ready at time of printing. Eds.

68

Almost Everything I Need To Know I Learned In Kindergarten

From the mouths of babes oftimes comes vomit.
—Brian Lam, publishing magnate

Planting the Seeds of Demotivation

The seeds of demotivation are planted at a very early age. Often, by contemplating our childhood—with its endless string of humiliations, defeats, fears and failures—we become more "in tune" with our less significant selves. In the following essay, "Sugar" Roy Carboyle reflects on his own childhood and its impact on his later development:

Almost everything I need to know I learned in kindergarten. For example, in Grade Four I learned a valuable safety lesson when our wiener dog Siegfried tried to mate with the next-door neighbour's Irish wolfhound. Then there was the time in Grade Six when our gym teacher Mr. Wooley came to class drunk, threw up on his sneakers, and was taken away in a police cruiser, never to be seen again. I think I learned something then.

But I think you know what I mean about kindergarten. Wisdom was not to be found at the top of the graduate-school mountain (although, I must admit, I came pretty close to wisdom once during reading break after a night on the beach with the McGuire twins), but there in the muck that passed for a sandpile outside my kindergarten class-room. It was a time of great innocence and wonder. These are the things I learned:

Share everything. That is, share everything so long as the teacher is watching. Because if Miss Katie catches you hogging toys, she'll take everything away and send you to the Hog Box, a cardboard container in the corner of the room, and you'll have to sit in it wearing a Styrofoam snout until naptime.

Play fair. In other words, don't cheat anymore than the next person. Adults call this "creating a level playing field."

Don't hit people. Least of all, people bigger and stronger than you. That's just plain stupid.

Put things back where you found them. And if you can't remember where you found them, sneak them into someone else's pile of stuff. Then it becomes their problem. Adults call this "delegating responsibility."

Don't sit beside the fat kid who smells funny.*

Say you're sorry if you hurt someone. Unless, of

---

* This comment is not meant to be construed as an attack on all large-sized children; many kids, of all body types, "smell funny." Eds.

course, you meant to hurt them. Then walk away briskly, with a satisfied smile on your face.

Stale cookies and lukewarm milk may not be the best, but you might as well get used to them; they're all you're going to get.

Take a nap every afternoon, preferably while the teacher is talking.

Hamsters and goldfish and even Siegfried the wiener dog—they all die. Just like that dead skunk we found on an class trip to the beach. Remember Miss Katie's words of warning: "Don't touch it! You might catch something."

Wash your hands before you eat, especially if you've just been to the beach.

Flush. Unless it's bigger than a hamster. Then bury.

Be aware of wonder. When you go out in the world, hold hands and stick together. Later, if you're alone and there's no parents around, quickly pull your pants down and show off your pee-pee.

If, heaven forbid, you get caught, always remember: *deny everything.*

As you can see, almost everything you need to know in life was learned in kindergarten. Unless, say, a tornado blows the roof off your house the day after your insurance expires. Or your wife runs off with that new aerobics instructor down at the health club. Or a Colombian border guard finds seven kilos of pure cocaine in your wooden leg. . . .

Actually, there's probably a lot of things in life that aren't covered by kindergarten. But you get the point. I mean, suppose we lived our adult lives by the rules we learned in

71

kindergarten? For one thing, there'd be no war. Nothing serious, anyway; nobody had any real good weapons in kindergarten. And wouldn't it be better if, instead of polluting our lakes or invading Third World countries, we just pulled our pants down and showed off our pee-pees?

And wouldn't it be a nicer world if we remembered to share things . . . other than diseases?

Just thinking about kindergarten brings back a flood of memories. Like the time I was rushed to the hospital to have my stomach pumped after eating too much mucilage, which was, in fact, a kind of glue and not a Swedish breakfast cereal like I thought. Or the day we all got to go home early because the new kid stabbed Miss Katie in the forehead with safety scissors after she took away all his toys and tried to stuff him in the Hog Box. Or when the entire class got scabies and mumps at the same time, and then Daddy got the mumps and his testicles swelled to the size of Mr. Potato Head, and he couldn't pass water for a week.

Actually. . . .

When you get right down to it, kindergarten wasn't such a great place after all.

Sorry for wasting your time.

Key Concepts

1. Childhood memories are fuzzy, at best.

2. While kindergarten has its good points, it also has its bad points.

3. Life is just one crushing defeat after another.

4. Sometimes authors add entire sections to a book, to artificially increase its length. This is called "padding your manuscript."

MENTAL EXERCISE 7:
Rediscovering Your Inner Child

Childhood memories are an endless source of anxiety, embarrassment and fear. Here are a few simple exercises to help you tap into this fountain of youthful misery, and rediscover the pathetic little crybaby that is your inner child.

1. Steal twenty dollars from your elderly mother's purse, then buy a bunch of candy and don't give her any.

2. Give the man beside you on the bus a noogie.

3. Run a red light, then start to cry when the cop gives you a ticket. Tell him you're sorry, and ask for a hug.

4. Slice open your hand with a circular saw, then ask the emergency room doctor to "kiss it better."

5. Go up to a biker in a bar and call him a "stupid idiot." Then run. Just before he catches you, stop dead and yell, "Times!"

6. Tell your boss that a dog ate the quarterly report.

7. At a business lunch, start to giggle for no particular reason, and keep laughing until you pass an entire wine spritzer through your nose.

8. While playing with matches, accidentally burn your house down. When the insurance adjuster comes over, start crying and ask him for a hug.

9. Ask the clerk in a department store to give you something for free. When she says no, lie down in the middle of the aisle screaming, crying and stomping your feet. Refuse to get up until the security guard gives you a balloon.

CHAPTER EIGHT

Men are from Mars, Dogs are from Pluto

You always get a second chance to make a bad impression.
—Jess Nichol, avant garde stock clerk

Cultivating Anxieties about Sex, Love and Relationships

Sex, marriage and relationships are the cash cows of demotivational psychology. Most of us are abysmal failures when it comes to matters of the heart; our romantic expectations wildly outstrip the realities of day-in day-out intimacy. Only a select few—serial killers, members of Congress—consider themselves successful lovers, leaving the rest of us to wallow in despair. "Sugar" Roy Carboyle, father of demotivational psychology and author of the very useful "medical" pamphlet *How to Drive Yourself Wild in Bed*, believes that sexual anxieties are "a healthy human expression." He refuses to elaborate on this point, though.

To enhance your natural sexual anxieties, here are a few excerpts from our upcoming home study video *The "You're Not As Good As You Think You Are©" Guide to Great Sex and Oriental Massage*. Watch as a parade of nubile young men and women "rub each other the wrong way," leading you by the hand, so to speak, through such classic massage techniques as "The Butterfly at the Gates of Hell," "The Yak and Flower Bed," "The Hummingbird Two Step" and the ever-popular "Soft Lens Close Up of a Young Man Manipulating A Woman's Pert Nipples." ($29.95. Must 18 years or older.)

Excerpt #1: Dressing Up.
After a hard day, it's always nice to treat yourself to something special. Start by relaxing in a hot bath; dim the lights, and take the phone off the hook. Then, why not slip into something sexy? A pair of black lace panties is a nice way to start, and why not try out that new brassiere, a special order from Victoria's Secret? Some fishnet stockings are a real turn-on—see how the seam creeps seductively up the back of your leg—and are best held up with French garters. To top it off, put on that new silk nightie. Now look at yourself in the mirror; say some positive things to yourself like, "Hey, I'm one sexy piece of flesh!" Now, hurry up and put that stuff away before your wife comes home.

Excerpt #2: Spontaneity.
Spontaneity is key to satisfying connubial relations. Interested couples should read Dr. "Sugar" Roy Carboyle's *Sexual Spontaneity: A Step-by-Step Guide.*

Excerpt #3: Location, Location, Location.

The *where* of sex is as important as the *how*, and certainly much more important than the *why*. We suggest couples take the time to choose the best possible environment. An ideal location is one that stimulates the Sexual Twin Towers of demotivational psychology: *fear* and *guilt*. Add an element of danger to your lovemaking: find some place where you might get caught. Of course, the final choice depends on your personality.

For a conservative couple, danger might mean making love with the bedroom door unlocked while the kids are still up. A more adventurous couple needs more stimulation; perhaps they will engage in sex play while on a mountain walk, or while watching an adult movie in a sparsely-crowded cinema. Some couples go even further. Madge and Eric would regularly have sex in the laundry room of their apartment building, and once managed a quickie during grace at their bridge club's annual Thanksgiving Luncheon.

In addition to an ideal locale, it's important to set the mood. At the outset of any activity, one partner should say, "We really shouldn't do this; what if we get caught?" Upon concluding, the other partner should sigh deeply then say, with great resolve, "We have to promise never to do this again."

Excerpt #4: Premature Ejaculation.

A common problem, occurring more frequently in men that in women. Interested couples should read Dr. "Sugar" Roy Carboyle's *Premature Ejaculation: A Step-by-Step Guide*.

Excerpt #5: Wife Swapping.

Only in dire cases of complete sexual incompatibility should anyone go to this extreme. We know of a couple who hadn't enjoyed intimate relations for seven years. We suggested they take drastic measures. The man swapped his wife. He got a new colour television and a collection of rare, first edition books. So far, both parties seem satisfied.

Excerpt #6: Size.

Yes. It is too small.

Key Concepts

1. Everyone has anxieties about sex.

2. We can't emphasize too strongly the importance of spontaneity in the maintenance of satisfying sexual relations.

3. Yes, your penis is, in fact, too small.

MENTAL EXERCISE 8:
Your Love Life: A Test

How unsuccessful is your love life? Take this little test to find out.

1. How many times a week do you make love?
   a) 3-5 times.
   b) 7-12 times.
   c) 7-12 times, sometimes more if I can find a partner.

2. What would you bring along on a first date?
   a) Chocolates and flowers.
   b) French wine, French bread, French safes.
   c) Rubber boots, eight gallons of cooking oil and three friends.

3. What do you think about oral sex?
   a) I'm against it; decent people don't do that sort of thing.
   b) It's a good thing; people should talk while they're making love.

4. What is your favourite position?
   a) Missionary.
   b) Man on bottom, wife in next room.
   c) That O.J. was "framed."

5. What to you think about phone sex?
   a) What two consenting adults choose to do is their own business.
   b) I have nothing against it, but it must be awfully uncomfortable.
   c) What two consenting phones choose to do is their own business.

6. How long does your average lovemaking session last?
   a) One to two hours.
   b) Ten to fifteen minutes.
   c) I'm not sure, I've never stayed awake long enough to find out.

7. What do you find sexy?
   a) Silk.
   b) Leather.
   c) Styrofoam.

8. What would say to your lover at the peak of passion?
   a) I love you!
   b) Don't stop!
   c) Hey, wake up!

9. What would you say afterwards?
   a) That was great.
   b) I love you.
   c) Are you finished yet?

10. What is your position on safe sex?
    a) Every adult should be responsible for their own sexual health.
    b) The government should take a role in supplying information.
    c) What two consenting safes do is their own business.

Score:
—1 point for every "a" answer
—5 points for every "b"
—10 points for every "c"

Rating:
10–20 points: Adequate love life; please re-read entire book.
20–30 points: Poor sex life; there's hope for you yet.
30 points +: Congratulations. You are an abysmal lover.

CHAPTER NINE

Aging Body, Endless Mortgage

God does not play dice with the universe.
Snooker, maybe, or Scrabble. But not dice.
—Albert Einstein's second cousin Gord

Squashing Your Spiritual Self

The process of demotivation is a spiritual journey. Ultimately, as we attain a higher degree of personal insignificance, we come to see the world as an empty chasm, a black hole in our hearts which sucks the very life force from us. This isn't necessarily a bad thing. It is, however, difficult to think of anything good to say about it. But no one coerced you into trying our patent-pending program. No one held a gun to your head and said, "Okay, you prick, read this book or I'll paint the walls a putrid shade of brain"—unless, of course, you ran into a particularly aggressive bookstore clerk. The point is, you made your bed, now lie in it. Quit complaining. Or, to put it in more scientific terms, Wake up! Smell the coffee!

Perhaps, one last story will help hammer home the point. It was told to us by a famous publisher who passed away several years ago, so there's no chance of him contradicting us.

Once, a young woman was riding the bus when an old man took the seat right beside her. Curiously enough, he was holding a bouquet in his hands. After a while, the old man struck up a conversation. He seemed to be marking time, really. Where, he asked the woman, do you work? What do you do there? Was she married, he wanted to know, and on hearing she was not, did she have any boyfriends? Did she enjoy dating? What kinds of things did she like to do on a date? Was she—he struggled to find the right word—promiscuous?

The young woman did not enjoy this line of questioning

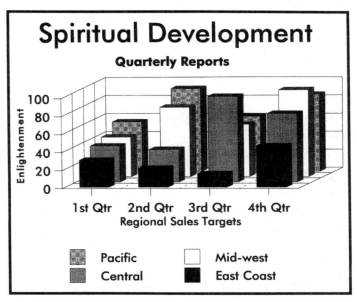

Figure 8: Spiritual Development.

at all. She asked the old man to move to another seat, and warned him if he didn't, she would complain to the bus driver.

The old man moved. But every once in a while, he caught the young woman staring at the bouquet of flowers he held in his wrinkled hands.

Eventually, the bus came to his stop, and just before the old man got off he did something wonderful. He walked over to the young woman. "I can tell that you like flowers. Here," he said, and handed the bouquet to her. "I'm sure my wife would like you to have them." His eyes twinkled and as he spoke the most bemused smile crossed his lips. Well, more a smirk than a smile, but the young woman let it pass.

The young woman accepted the flowers graciously. Her eyes followed the old man as he got off the bus and . . . proceeded directly through the gates of the nearby cemetery.

But wait. That's not the end of the story. For, as the bus pulled away, the young woman caught one last glimpse of the old man emerging from the graveyard. He had a fresh bouquet of flowers in his hands! She was aghast. He was stealing flowers from the graveyard to give to unsuspecting women on the bus!

This touching and somewhat perverted story serves to remind us of several things. First, the graveyard reminds us that, sooner or later—probably sooner—we all die. From this, there is no escape. No amount of booze or pills or facelifts or hair transplants or testicle tucks or liposuction or cheery advice from high-priced self-help experts can halt Death's relentless march to your door. It's pretty depressing when you think about, actually. But that's life.

Second, this story shows us how bus travel, while fairly cost effective and environmentally friendly, often puts us in contact with a host of undesirable people. A general rule of thumb: avoid public transit whenever possible.

Key Concepts
The Book In Review

1. Successful people are less happy.

2. Your brain is your own worst enemy.

3. Using defirmations, we can train our mind to create and reinforce a negative perception of the world.

4. The art of setting self-defeating goals is a core concept to both demotivational psychology and most urban planning committees.

5. The Win/Whine Paradigm is one of the most important intellectual breakthroughs of the century, which is quite pathetic when you think about it.

6. Indecision and procrastination are the "twin towers" of demotivational wisdom.

7. Childhood is highly overrated.

8. Every sexual and personal relationship you've ever had was doomed to failure from the start.

9. When you think about it, these *Key Concepts* are just another way to pad the book.

10. Eventually, we all die, so quit your blubbering.

Pushing Yourself To The Limit: A Personal Challenge From The Authors

Congratulations. By now, you should be well on your way toward leading a less successful and satisfying life. We hope that such demotivational concepts as Goal Overload, the Win/Whine Paradigm and the Hidden Wisdom of Indecision and Procrastination—along with our powerful, patent-pending defirmation technique—will knock you down a notch, will bring you back to Earth and then some.

But let's not stop there. We challenge you to go the next step, and you can start by picking up the phone. Pick it up right now. We dare you. No. We *double* dare you.

Call our toll-free hot line, 1-888-600-SUKS. That's 1-888-6-0-0-S-U-K-S. Order a second copy of *You're Not As Good As You Think You Are*© to put away for safekeeping in case you lose this copy.

And while we've got you on the line, order ten more copies of the book. By why stop at ten? We challenge you to order twenty—no, twenty-five copies of the book, to give out to friends, relatives and acquaintances, or simply to hoard in your basement to bear mute witness to the impending Armageddon. Are you up to our challenge? Do you have the right stuff to meet this difficult sales objective? Because if you are "up to it," then in your own small way, you're a kind of hero. Someone the rest of the community can look to for inspiration and leadership. If you're not up to this challenge then you are zero. Hero, or zero? The choice is yours.

Operators are standing by.

ABOUT THE AUTHORS

According to his business card, "Sugar" Roy Carboyle is "the world's foremost expert on demotivational psychology." A former Olympic Games volunteer and short order cook, he is currently working on his memoir, *I've Got To Hand it To Me: My Seven Years of Involuntary Celibacy*. He has been married six times, and has four or five wonderful children.

Chris Gudgeon is a best-selling author in his native country of Canada, "The Belgium of the Americas." He's contributed to numerous magazines, including *Mad*, *National Lampoon* and *The West Coast Dog Fancier's Mange Support-Group Newsletter*. He is learning to live with success.

ALSO AVAILABLE FROM ARSENAL PULP PRESS

Death Writes *Darlene Barry Quaife*
Griffin and Sabine's evil twin: Death's personal notebook, in which Death opines on the ways of the living.
$11.95 Cda/$9.95 U.S.

Silence Descends *George Case*
An imagined history of the next 500 years, depicting the end of the Information Age.
$11.95 Cda/$9.95 U.S.

Scrambled Brains *Konstabaris & LeBlanc*
A cooking guide for the reality impaired: those low on funds but high on attitude. Scramble on!
$16.95 Cda/$14.95 U.S.

Higher Grounds *Kevin Barefoot, ed.*
The Little Book of Coffee: quotations, definitions and statistics on everyone's favorite beverage.
$4.95 Canada and U.S.

Blood Lines *Barb Stewart, ed.*
The Little Book of Vampires: trivia, lore and quotations, shedding light on this darkest of horror legends.
$4.95 Canada and U.S.

These and other Arsenal Pulp Press titles are available through your local bookstore, or directly from the press (with Visa or Mastercard) by calling **1-888-600-PULP**.

Or send a cheque or money order (add postage: $3.00 for first book, $1.50 per book thereafter; Canadian residents add 7% GST) to:

ARSENAL PULP PRESS
103-1014 Homer Street
Vancouver, B.C. Canada
V6B 2W9

Write for our free catalogue.